Overall politics can truly be a confusing thing to be a part of. In modern day times however, more and more people are getting into local politics for many reasons. With an ever changing political climate and members of all political parties in the US having a seemingly endless task set we decided this would be a great tool to help people learn the new way to politics.

Since the age of 13 I have been working on campaigns from Presidential to local school boards and more I have seen a lot. My mother and step father from a very young age had a major influence on my goals in life and now almost exactly 20 years after they were running an organization so am I. With this being stated I wrote this guide / book in hopes that it helps you and or your candidates succeed.

Thank You,
Brandon Harris

Intro: What all goes into a campaign Online?

Managing a campaign of any size can be a really daunting task. In today's world of the internet and politics life seems to catch us by surprise and we're seeing a ton of changes in our political culture. Both Democrats and Republicans are taking to an online platform to build their campaigns and better their chances of winning their race. This method has become so influential it's scary.

Just recently it was stated to congress that Google swayed a suggested 10,000,000 votes in Hillary Clinton's direction in the 2016 election cycle with their search engine. It's also widely assumed that our current POTUS Donald Trump won because of Russian online meddling though it has never been factually proven. Either way the use of social media, websites, blogs and search engines is essential in the current world of politics.

In 2018, I was able to prove a theory that utilizing all assets of online marketing over an extended period can and will increase your overall chances of winning an election and with the help of a good friend and solid politician Jim Dodge we were able to do just that. By planning and networking our approach down to a science we took a statewide campaign for Illinois state treasure to a whole new level. See Jim decided to run in one of the hardest Republican years possible in Illinois and he as well as myself and our partner Dean Casper decided to start working together in June of 2018 already well into Jim's campaign. This relationship was fresh and it took some real learning for all of us but we were able to come out of the race well more educated than any of us had ever believed. This lead us to the following list of what goes into a campaign online!

What All Do I Need?

- A Quality Website

- Social Media Presence

- A Donation Source

- A Lot of Videos

- SEO

- A Network

- A Click Team

- Set Goals Data Analytics

- Some Common Knowledge

So as you may have guessed already that is how we are going to structure this book each of the first 9 chapters will cover exactly what is needed and how to plan, build and utilize these tools for success. If at any point you get lost or confused simply stop and retrace the previous chapter and the steps we lay out in this book!

Chapter 1: The Concept

We all have a pre developed concept. Whether it's a campaign, candidate or cause, every person has a reason for looking at this book. Your concept is huge. Pre-developed concepts are huge. Having a pre-developed concept is always great but can definitely use to be tweaked. Our concepts are always in need of shaping and forming. If you can shape and form your pre developed concept, that leaves you the ability to shift the good and bad from your concept and build a perfect idea.

Building your thoughts into a plan is a necessity to form a successful online campaign for your candidate or campaign. From start to finish you must ensure your concept meets the necessary qualities to reach the peaks you wish for it to reach. From the plan to the colors, mood, and emotion. Our concept is our base, with our base we have the ability to further our planning. If we per se have a blog about politics but only wish to reach an audience of female voters between the ages of 18 - 35 we would not want part of our concept to be covering topics relating to men such as a new law forcing male birth control. Yes I know that is an out there statement but it is being used in a seance to show a concept flaw. We always want to ensure our concept reachers are targeted viewers and potential voters or donors.

Our voters or donors and Viewer base is well planned and developed in this stage. It does not matter if you're a fan based blog, or a business looking to profit, you have to know whom your target market is. If you have no target and are all over the place you will not reach the goals of success. Social media and online business success are not achieved through hail Mary passes, well at least not often, but rather through strategic planning and follow through. Your concept will be essential in the follow through of your plan.

Our concept should start very simple, a name, a mission and an end goal. No this does not mean you have to end it in 2040, all I am saying is that you must simply have an end goal in mind for a period of time. Even if it is within say a 12 month period, as long as you have and end for the first goal you have something to work towards!

Once you have a name a mission and a goal you are now on the path to lay out your target. You target is what you will be aiming for through your whole journey. This is a journey by the way, development is a journey, a s is success.

Your concept is a base of everything, I hit on it so hard because it took me years to develop my first successful concept. I had a vague Idea, but the actual concept and passion I put into it gave me the fire to continue my journey. Once you have developed a concept your mind constantly wishes to tweak and change, you will know you are on the path to success.

We all have that fire, that want to succeed but very few of us gun for it with a fiery passion. Once you have come up with this and put it into planning you will know when it is what you are passionate about. No matter what this will lead you to success. This will be your sure fire way to ensure you do not give up on yourself. If we do not give up on ourselves we are almost guaranteed the ability to at least have a shot at the successful numbers we wish to reach.

On the next page is a chart on how to base your concept follow the chart, and really think for a while. Once you have your mind set on what you are going to do we can move onto the next chapter of the book.

Meaning of Name:

Name:_______________________________

____

____

____

Goal:

____

____

____

____

____

____

Target Market:

____

____

____

____

Social outlets:

____

____

____

____

____

____

Demographics:

____

____

____

____

____

____

The worksheet above will help you to know what you are about and who you are working to bring to your campaign site. This will be your working base for the next few chapters. Success is much easier to reach once you have these things all built into your concept. Each of us choose to build differently but as long as your concept is strong you can build from here.

Chapter 2: Planning

Planning your campaign or candidate efforts is not just slam bam thank you and get going. This process takes time, research and good decisions. What are your goals? Where do you want to be in the next 6 or 12 months? These are things to take into consideration when you are developing your plan. You also need to think about brand awareness. Your candidate or campaign brand, your name is that brand. This is all branding at some point or another.

Your online campaign is an extension of your campaign or candidate essentially and it represents you and the other people involved. You have to take pride in what you do and build on it to truly succeed in life! Planning with anything you do is important, but planning for your business marketing and success will lead you in the right direction. What do you want the end result to be? What are your goals? How many donors can you generate and what do you have to spend to get there? These are all questions you must ask yourself and your team in the planning stage.

Sitting down and writing a marketing plan is essential. Having a content plan to go with it is a must too. Developing a base around what it is that you are trying to do will give you structure and foundation. Get a pen and paper sit down and write following the following structure.

Section 1: Executive Summary

Develop your executive summary. Who are you and what is your campaign or candidate about? What makes you stand out from the rest? Define your campaign and or candidate and your goals.

Section 2: Target voters or donors

Who are the voters or donors you are trying to reach? What is their income level? Where are they located? What attributes do they have?

(Sample) voters 35 or older with an income of $50,000 a year. Individuals who are homeowners but are undecided on 2020 election.

Section 3: Unique Selling Proposition (USP)

What is your unique selling point? What makes your campaign or candidate stand out? Figure out exactly what it is that sets your campaign and or candidate apart and run with it!

Now once you are done with the planning section we are going to get a lot more in depth. We will cover what software you will need in the next chapter. Yes I said software. Don't be scared by this there is a lot of free stuff out there that can be used as well as a lot of reasonable pricing.

Chapter 3: Your Website

A website is the most essential tool your campaign will have unless you have the ability to reach 3000 or even 300 Million voters. Your website will lead to a lot of great things in your direction if built and utilized properly. Your site will be where users can find things like your online donations, sign up information and much more.

Where should I get my site is probably crossing your mind right now if you don't know a designer or know how to build one yourself. We hear this question a lot and we often suggest if you have no experience hire a professional for your first site. This may make or break your campaign in the future. Having a pro help is never bad and you can feel 100% free to use the set up guide we offer below.

Website Set Up Guide

We have found that no matter the race or size of the race having a focused breakdown is essential. We highly suggest you start with the following pages:

Home:

Give your users a simple but solid home page. You want a picture of the candidate, a clear description of the office you or your candidate are seeking a video, donate link, social media links and a contact form. You will also need a paid for disclaimer at the bottom depending on your state laws or if your candidate is under the federal board of elections.

About:

This is where the candidate shines. Explain a bit about your candidate. Use this section to express background, family and history in the community. If you utilize this section properly it should bring your viewers into your site even hold them. Be through and be sure to link other pages well.

Platform:

Your platform page should be filled with top of the line breakdown of what it is that you stand for and why. This is where you can target your key issues and really let voters know what it is that you stand for and believe in. If done right this page could very well sway voters. Be 100% sure you are very focused and that you educate voters properly. Make sure your stance is sheerly known on this page.

Donations:

Develop a donations page. No matter if your using Paypal or another service you will be able to use this page to give users a place to give online donations. If utilized properly you can surly entice some donors on this page. I highly recommend placing a video on this page of you talking to the voters! This can increase online donations by as much as 11%.

News:

This page should be links of any media coverage your campaign has received. Often as the campaign season progresses you will get written about in the local media. Use this page to highlight any positive press attributes. This will not only provide positive attention and credibility but also backlinks for your website which help with SEO.

Videos:

On this page you will link all videos of you and or your campaign team. This page will also be an amazing resource for you as 85% of all voters use their phones for information and more than 90% make decisions based on video in today's world.

Local Resources:

This is a personal touch I began doing around 2009 to make my candidates websites really stand out from the rest. By providing a resources page you are leading more traffic to your site and helping the constituents in your district.

I suggest links to things like food pantry, tax assessor's office, court house, local family out reach, local drug treatment center etc. This will really help to have local resources and you can even use it as a marketing piece.

Blog:

A blog can become your best asset in your campaign if used properly. Each post acting as a fishing hook with a fresh worm for the search engines like Google, Bing and Yahoo. If you use these post properly and build a brand and following with them you will see a huge traffic increase on your website over a period of time.

If you build the following and brand it will lead you to a very successful build of followers. You should be posting things like " Sue May for Congress Helps Build Local Garden" or "Debate Highlights From Debate". Be sure to use catchy titles and be very focused on the quality of your content. By doing so you will ensure optimal traffic results. A good blog has a clear balance of content, interactive materials, videos and comments! Believe it or not some of our politicians in Illinois and other states for that matter have seen amazing results on their election from social media and shared blog post. This is the way of future politics. If you utilize the skills at hand and build a quality base and consistent flow of content your blog will gain and maintain a growing base. This could be great for this election or overall for your future aspirations

If you utilize all of these pages suggested above and build a site that is both desktop and mobile friendly you will see amazing results. You should also be thinking about the mechanics of your campaign website and what exactly you expect it to provide for you and your campaign.

Make a Website Plan

Develop a solid plan of action for your campaign website. As most people do not realize the potential their website offers, they often do not think to build and follow a plan for success. Simply building a plan or hiring a professional to utilize this tool for you is an amazing idea. Your goal sheet should include the following:

- **Donation Goals**

A. How you're going to target donors.

B. Why these donors will donate to you.

C. When you plan to meet your goals

D. Total donation goal

- **Viewer Count Goals**

A. Total viewer count

B. Viewer count broken down by age and voting record.

C. Email newsletter sign up count

- **Retention Time**

A. How long your viewer stays on the site.

B. What pages you want to hold viewers longest

C. Content goals to pull in viewers

Simple goals for your website like these above will help you to better define a goal for your site development team and will also give you benchmarks for your success.

If done right your website can turn into the best tool you have next to your social media accounts. Combined the two have proven worthy of helping to win campaigns all over the nation.

You must also think deeper than building with your website. Your logo and your brand are key to your success. People need to know who you are. If I were running I would use my name on my own site 3 times or more on each page. I use an old trick I developed with long tail keywords.

Long Tail Keyword trick for website

Ensure you are placing your Long Tail keywords properly. By not doing so you're losing valuable traffic to your website. Keep focused and be sure to keep track of details for your keywords as well.

Will County Board Brandon Harris

Brandon Harris for Will County Board

Brandon Harris For Congress in Illinois

Using the above samples as an idea for your Long-tail keywords you can make your own sources of traffic to your campaign website. For over 12 years I have grown and learned and watched as the online world went from barely breaking the surface to dominating the campaigns we see today.

If you can develop a website with great SEO and an amazing blog you can and will see points gained like never seen before. The internet is of huge value to your campaign and should be an essential top tool for building your success. We will also cover keywords more in chapter 4 as well.

Always Add A Blog

So we all have heard the overwhelming term SEO. For a lot of people it's simply mumbo jumbo they just don't get. To break this down we decided to go over exactly what SEO is and why it will boom if you have a blog on your campaign site.

SEO (search engine optimization) is a loosely used term for tightening up your website to search engines liking. So in essence you need to follow proper practices. There is a lot that goes into SEO but over time it can be built up to dominate Google and other search engines if done right. This is part of the reason why we say that having a blog is essential. See a blog is usually an update board in your site for your campaign. Videos and pictures as well as designed and written content can be essential.

If you update your blog regularly overtime the search engine spiders AKA bots that read your site and judge where it belongs in the listing rank will index new post. The more quality posts you have, the more likely you index better.

What Is A Blog?

A blog is a collection of articles, pictures and videos where you can place your thoughts, materials, stances and events all in one place. I have found over the years that your blog can be the best thing you can do for yourself and your goals if you really put your time into it.

Blogging is something like writing a journal but online on your website.

How Often Should I Blog?

You should blog daily if possible. If you have a marketing team or campaign your using for your campaign you can also ask for them to keep it up and moving. The more often you drop quality blog post with a consistent pattern, the more likely you will be to succeed.

How Do I Create website Content Voters Will Pay Attention To?

This part is easy.simply use things like memes, infographics and issues to build your brand. If your content is engaging such as a funny Meme it could take off rather quickly. Below is a list of post types labeled from 1st to last.

How Do I Even Create A Blog?

If you have no Idea what a blog is or how they work it's pretty simple to get this tool planned and developed. You can actually use something like Wix, Wordpress or Godaddy to create a site and add a blog to your site.

Adding a blog or posting section is essential to growing your online campaign. To do so you can simply contact your website provider and ask for them to help you add a blog or if your up for it you could also check out my site and I will walk you through it. My domain is www.brandonharris.org.

List Of Content Types

memes - each meme shared 5 times usually reaches 2000 in reach and can be great.

Infographics

Infographics are an amazing way to get traffic to your website. These tools can gain traction and help you focus viewers in on targeted issues.

Vlogs

A vlog or better known as informational video that is kind of like a blog can really help you to grow an online presence for your campaign. People love this type of content. It not only allows them to get a better grasp of your personality but also it allows them to see and hear directly from you as a person and candidate.

Chapter 4: Have A Social Media Presence

Social media is a complex and interesting world. Knowing social media is like knowing which way the wind blows. Trends are interesting and always changing. Social media trends often get lost before you know it and switching up your flow to keep up with the tide is a task. I am a campaign minded person who eats, sleeps, and breathes social media. Honestly I have made a great portion of my living via social media and I know it better than most. If there is a trend to keep up with I'm there and through this process I learned exactly how to use social media as a tool to my advantage and there is a lot of work that goes into this step. It also pours into campaigning well.

Social media is a complex organism. Learning social media and understanding the in's and out's. With social media you can choose many different channels to success. I choose to use what I call the " Blitz It" method. With my method I use as many social outlets as possible. I build each page with a similar look and build. Consistency is key. Having a consistent look and feel is important. If you have a look everyone is familiar with you are what is called in the marketing world branded. Branding your campaign and or candidate it may be you are building is huge! Branding what it is that you are working on will give you a name, the consistent look will give you a wholesome feel. Once you have this mastered it's time to start the content development portion of the work.

Your content, meaning post, pictures, blog articles, anything on the internet you must have quality content. If you do not have top of the line content it will be very hard to succeed at whatever it is you want to succeed. You need top of the line content. From the subject to the art work, everything in your content must be pristine, Top of the line content equals ensured viewer retention. Viewers are interested in content that they like, understand, and that is quality. If you can reach a viewer and retain them you have officially won. This is what we're all after. Whether you want them to buy something from you, or read something you have written, viewer retention equals success. Your content has got to stand out as much as your concept. Take time developing your content. Even down to the wording this can be crucial when developing content you wish to have social media success with your campaign.

Social Media is based off of a really interesting thing called algorithms. An algorithm is basically a mathematical formula that social media companies use these algorithms to assess your page activity and flow. They like to see consistency. So if you post say three times on your page one day, 5 times the next, and fifteen the day after that is very inconsistent. You are better off to post three times a day for 6 weeks and see how that pattern works for your social media sites. By doing so you will have shown consistency for a long enough period of time that the we can be sure the systems have read you as consistent, and your numbers will begin to rise. This pattern will show you over a period of time great results. I personally always try to build onto my pattern, I use a cool site called hootsuite and I change every 6 weeks adding more post into my plan. So say today until six weeks from now I was doing 3 post a day. In six weeks I would sit down, re cap and rebuild that plan. I may now do 5 post a day for six weeks and so on. This is a building process but it can surely help you build into the numbers you are attempting to reach.

Once you have a pattern, a design, and quality content the next big step is keeping up with your base. I have often used email list and admin on my social media pages to do these jobs. If you only receive a handful of messages a day, then there is no need for another admin as long as you are sure you can handle the flow of your pages, site, or blog. Once you begin to gain large amounts of followers I would suggest you pick up at least one other admin to help. This will ease the stresses you have on you managing one or multiple applications. It will also allow for prompt responses to questions and concerns. Email list can also be extremely useful. Using a quality email list can ensure your clients, viewers, or voters or donors see new things going on and also when you post. If you keep your viewers informed they tend to come back. As a blog reader, or even a site viewer I like to know what's going on, what's new, and so on. Keeping up with your base is an essential step. If you do not you will lose them. I will say again consistency, consistency, consistency… I want to make sure I drill that in if you do not stay consistent you will fail no matter what. Once you fall off so will your followers. That is bad for you and campaign. You must keep things regular and people entertained. Doing so is a huge responsibility of anyone running social media platforms.

Social media Spam is huge. I do not suggest getting yourself listed as a spammer. This can really affect your overall reach and effectiveness. If you want to reach a million people today, you're in the wrong place, you might as well quit reading this book. I am 100% against spam campaigns, they do not help anyone, and they make the job of social media people harder and harder every day. Spam or smear campaigns are for people who cannot get traction because their content is lacking. If you are spamming you are falling. Do not host 20 events on Facebook a month to build onto your page. One I have no issue with, but 20, that is excessive and showing weakness as a campaign, blog, or site. It will also have your url, or social page links marked as spam. This is a huge No, no you do not want. Once they have you flagged it is extremely hard to redeem yourself.

Social site development, blog development, and even website development are fairly hard tasks. Yes they do take time to complete.

Following this book you will be well on your way. But always remember that spam is not the answer. Do you ever open your email to find that one annoying email letter you didn't sign up for? What do you do with it? You either put it directly in the trash bin, or mark it as spam. No matter what you are spamming from spam is toxic to you as a campaign person. Spam has killed millions of blogs, sites, and amazing Facebook pages and groups. Forced adds often fail as well. Also buying likes, and views is a failing game. It's a short term leap but people are not blind. If you have 600,000 likes on a page and 2 comments per post, you're a fraud. We see this all the time. Hard work and honesty in this world get you a lot farther!

There are a ton of social media sites out there as well. From Facebook, Twitter, Mocospace, Meetme, Instagram, Pinterest, Linkedin and hundreds of others. Each site offers different things, so be sure to check out all sites available. Some sites may offer things others do not. Each service is worth a look, the internet is complex but these sites are all useful tools. I would suggest using each tool to your advantage and seeing what works best for you personally. For each person this may be different but well worth the shot!

As though it's not enough that facebook has a million different tools, even creating proper ads and artwork can be a challenge. When developing proper ad's and marketing pieces you have to think like your voter If you don't you will fail and I can guarantee that. Our voters or donors bases are so used to being drowned with Less than quality content. You have to develop this content and turn it into the turnpike of your campaign. If you are not using your Own channels for marketing, and not building a base you are letting yourself down.

In today's day and time it is highly important you build your name brand on social media. If you don't already have a plan putting one together could be the make or break for your campaign. When we look in recent history if we go back to 2002 Democrat Howard Dean utilized this as a tool first. Creating online meet ups the team were able to reach about 140,000 people with online meet ups in the 2002 cycle. Then on 2004 Mark Zuckerberg served as a field director on the John Kerry for President campaign, the same year Facebook was founded. Mark was responsible for the get out to vote mobilization and through the use of the baby platform it did well. Again in 2016 we saw near 36% of people learn about candidates via social media. Thus having a proper presence is essential!

Building your personal brand is key to getting voters attention at little to no cost. For instance I started building my own brand back when Google plus was essential. In late 2019 utilizing my brand as well as a few other locals we were capable of reaching over 100 Million people online with our Boycott Walmart push that went national. You as a candidate should do the same. It is definitely an uphill process but if done right it can pan out very well for you and your campaign!

Where do I start with My Social Building?

Well this question all depends on where you are at with your social media to begin with. I know I have meet candidates at all ages who use social media daily, and those who hate it all together. It all comes down to what assets online you already have, and what you can develop among your staff and your own skills. If you can do it the following layout is key. If not feel free to contact a professional.

Social Media Map

First Tier:	*Second Tier:*	*Third Tier:*
Facebook	YouTube	Whats App
Twitter	Linked-In	Snap Chat
Instagram	Reddit	

Each of These tiers are essential for a complete online social media campaign and plan. Your first tier being Facebook, Twitter and Instagram. If each tier is properly developed your campaign could potentially reach 85% of your voter base at ¼ of the cost. Campaign has for many years been a sport of many dollars spent and mass coverage, in today's world mass precision is key!

On the next page we will list each platform and exactly what they are useful for! Be sure to check them out and see exactly how each can help your campaign for office.

Facebook:

First we need to look at the sheer facts here. Facebook was created and launched in February of 2004 and has become the main super power in the world of social media. With an estimated 2.4 Billion weekly users worldwide.

This tool alone is a masterpiece. From personal experience on a small local level we have used this tool as recently as 2019 reaching 100 million voters in a period of 30 days. You as a campaign should utilize this as well. Below we are going to layout our plan and concept for growth with a campaign.

Facebook Campaign Set Up:

A. Main candidate page

B. City, neighborhood, county or state support pages.

C. City, neighborhood, county or state support groups

D. Mass use support header images

How do I set this up?

You first set up your candidate page. If this is a struggle you can hire a professional but if you are in tune or have a volunteer to help get this step out of the way first. Then move into the support pages.

Support Page Breakdown

These pages will break down different targeted areas of your district to focus on targeted issues. In let's say New Lenox, Illinois you target middle class voters with an income of $200,909 a year your issues will be a lot different than in Winetka, Illinois where you're targeting upper class voters with an average income of $989,816 a year.

Your team needs to be diligent when utilizing these tools to prepare your campaign for success. You need to know your voters about as well as they know themselves as targeted voter data is essential.

Support Page Breakdown Management

Support page break down should be managed by campaign staff and if possible a local volunteer. It is essential that you break down the chain of command and get in a solid schedule with content distribution. This will help maximize your reach and ultimately help ensure your message is properly shared and heard.

Support Group Breakdown

This Breakdown will be a little different than the support page Breakdown. We want to utilize the pages with very strict targeting and with the groups though we should be picky we can be a a bit more lenient on how we target. As groups can grow much quicker than pages and even have skyrocketed interactions we will develop these with a different twist. Of course we will remain focused on targeted areas and issues such as "People for Cleaner Water Standing With Harris" or " Will County Citizens for Harris" but when it comes to new members we can make these groups public with a few base questions to join. We can also utilize these to move through our voter base quickly and with a bit of hard work we can have a well built stable of social warriors and interested voters in no time.

Support Group Breakdown Management

Support group breakdown management is also the same as support management but I often get as many local leaders that are with my cause into the group as managers and admins. The more people you have active in your group the more likely it will rank higher in local group searches. This will help with the overall social reach and SMO over a period of time. If you like many others are wondering what SMO is it is Social Media Optimization and or the ability to utilize overall ground coverage and quality to appeal to the social media spiders thus taking your groups to another level completely.

Why Do I Need Ads?

So you have a campaigns and candidates facebook page? That's great! But that page honestly is valueless unless you know how to use it. Using Facebook ads can be a daunting task. Often you're unsure of what to do, or how to go about using the ads. There are a million how to guys on the market promising you the world. Let's be honest, it is not all that simple. People bring you in with the promise of .1 cent ads and expect you to jump loops. We know differently. We as a team have been very successful with social media. The facebook advertising platform can be extremely challenging. Our plans and cycles are a bit extreme. We work at our goals relentlessly. But if you follow the quick plan below you will be greatly impacted for the better.

1. Use the analytics software built into your facebook to learn a few things.
    i. Optimal Online time.
    ii. Age and Sex.
    iii. Find your most recourse full information.

2. Develop content that will entertain the minds of your target market. I always build my content around my target market.

3. Use your ad settings. Set your target market. When you're setting you areas you want the ad to be seen. The more precise you are the better off you are.

4. Do not buy fans or followers on facebook. Campaigns and candidates assume they must have a lot of followers to sell on Facebook and that is not the case. To make a direct impact on your Facebook you must pay for ads and develop an organic following.

It doesn't matter if you are a political candidate and campaign, growth always needs to be organic, and built through content and your brand.

Why can't I get responses on my campaign or candidates post?

When making a facebook post you have to think like the person you are selling to. Your post and backlinks have to be clever and precise. Delivering a message to a consumer or even another business is already tricky enough online. We often build and develop adds that are all about our products all the time. If that is what you are doing, stop while you're ahead. Branding yourself and building on Facebook you must develop a proper plan that allows you to be real, and grow. I will not buy a product from someone who fills my notifications with their sales pitch. I would more than likely block them and stray away from those people. While building your base you should do attention catching post. Yes, you still should sponsor ads and work hard to build the reach of your post as well. Below is an add I did recently that went very well.

By directly targeting your ads you are developing an easier way to speak with your base. If you want them to listen, you must take you 1 second of attention you will receive and make them bite. This will ensure that you have a better chance than most of your add being viewed and or clicked. When developing an add for a base of voters or donors or past voters or donors on facebook it is highly important that you know the who and what of what you are preparing these ads. Developing these add's is one thing, making them have any return, let alone maximum reach is a whole different story.

To develop top of the line adds is a bit of a task. You must be able to build a plan and follow through with it as well. Learning your base is a daunting task but you can use facebook ad google analytics to help you get the job done. For instance if your selling lawn care and your online base is 15-25 with an income level of $20,000 a year, you are in the wrong place. You must develop a base of content that meets the needs of your voters or donors. This is what will bring the best voters or donors base.

Helpful hint:

Keep an Excel or Google Drive file with all of the groups and pages to ensure your getting maximum reach over all!

Twitter:

Twitter is another extremely useful tool that can help you with your campaign though it no longer allows political ads. As a campaign or candidate you can utilize this tool to succeed but due to modern day political culture you will have to be more careful with exactly how this is done. If you post on Twitter and build a following you would be surprised on how the following could actually help you! Twitter is one of the top social media sites for engagement and unlike many of their competitors they offer a really clean and professional atmosphere.

Twitter Hashtags:

Utilizing hashtags on twitter is essential! If you really get into the use of relevant hashtags you will succeed quicker than expected on twitter! Now if as hashtag is an uncommon term to you we wanted to be sure you knew what a hashtag was so we decided to break it down a bit for you.

What Is A Hashtag?

A hashtag is a word or phrase with the pound symbol directly attached to the word or phrases. If you're attempting to utilize a phrase or multiple words in a hashtag you cannot leave space between the words, letters or the hashtag with the first letter.

Sample Hashtags:

#conservativememes #rightwing #election #patriot #constitution #liberty #government #libtards #memes #meme #walkaway #news #a #guns #hillaryclinton #whitehouse #nra #fakenews #trumpsupporters #american #truth #republicanparty #republicanmemes #liberals #obama #proudamerican #capitalism #redpill #hillaryforprison #freespeech

Instagram:

Instagram is a great platform that offers the user a great way to reach voters. Instagram has 1 billion monthly users across the globe and it has continued to grow! Instagram when properly set up can offer you a solution to reaching voters across the nation! If you utilize this tool with the insight features you can really narrow in and target your traffic at a much better rate than other social media sites.

Instagram utilizes a different social exchange than most other platforms as well. With a slew of photos and videos it allows you to build a follower base with photos and videos but no backlinks in the post or videos. This method allows users to utilize videos and images to ensure they are engaging followers!

If used well you can build a large and focused following on instagram through consistent posing over a period of time. If you utilize this platform the results can be amazing. I had my first experience with this taking my own brand with my name to 31,100 followers over a 1 and a half year period of time. I got there with simple focus on the content I was sharing, as well I kept a clear simple track from what was working. I kept a tracker and within 6 months I was over 15,000 followers. This turned an engagement of roughly 50,000 users a month. You as a campaign manager or candidate can utilize a tracker to keep an eye on your results. After each month if you focus in on the post either video and or images and hash tags that work best you can succeed even more!

Chapter 5: Breaking the ice

When you launch any sort of social media campaign you must break the ice. It is of the highest importance that you break the ice and ensure your are capable of reaching as many individuals as possible while being socially active in hopes you gain a follower and a possible donor or voter. If you're horrible with communication, then you shouldn't even be to this point in the book. A lot of what you are doing here is playing a double persona here, no not in a psychological way but more so in an effort to learn and understand the people you are attempting to reach. If you want to break the ice, you must first have a goal and base that you are looking to meet. If you do not then your chances of failing are high. There are a list of things you must do to break the ice. I will take you step by step in this chapter to make sure you meet these expectations!

1. Development

Developing a social media platform is now day's much like designing a website. By setting up a solid and well planned out page you are much more likely to stand out than you competition. Developing your pages means fully filling out your campaign page or listing and ensuring it is fully functional. If you do this it will greatly increase your flow of traffic. Our traffic flows from other sources as well as ourselves building a few different steps into a combination of success. When you complete all of your online profiles correctly you can also increase your traffic by almost 30%.

2. Page post

Please always remember when posting on social media that this is not your website or a place to focus on selling. Yes we all want to reach our market and sell our products, but we also must remember that our post must be meaningful and useful or we will fail. A lot of campaigns and candidates attempt to use their social media pages as a home for poorly made ad's. To be honest this is not a sales platform whatsoever. Unless your ultimate goal is to push traffic away you must use your social media pages as just that. Be social, interact with followers. If you interact and provide your followers with great new content you can grow your base in a smooth and effective way. No this does not mean build the boat and they will come, you will have to market your pages and product to build your own base. If you use these pages appropriately they will help you grow your base and voters in no time at all.

3. Tapping Your Base

When working to tap your base, w e will have generally assumed you have created and provided quality content for your viewers. By doing so you are developing an active following. If you can get them listening and opening messages you can and will succeed. Your base is derived by a group of alike people that follow you do to something your content does for them. If you write about lawn care, they may be looking for a solution to an issue, or a new product. If you're a musician, you may provide leisure time and comfort to a base. But no matter what it is that you are doing you are in need of getting your base of followers to participate when breaking the ice. Do you ever see pictures with 1000 or 2000 Shares on facebook, or the image on IG with 5000 Likes? It is a daunting image in mosts minds until they themselves are capable of creating this type of following. Using the base you have you can create this level of success and much more through the proper use of social media marketing!

Each of these steps will help lead you into a proper formatting for your online life. By mastering each of these steps you will be capable of creating a web online. This web will all work towards one essential goal, more views and voters on your site! Using the breaking the Ice stage to truly add character and a sense of fullness to your social profiles will leave you feeling complete and also will give you a must higher traffic base due to properly managed and up-kept profiles.

As you develop and get through the ice breaking stage you will come to find that once thought impossible goals become more and more simple to obtain. Per se today if you have 1000 followers, if you follow this plan and work through the pains you will have 5000 in 8 months. This is if you follow this plan and work it correctly. A lot of the development you are leading to is website traffic, and from there email list and information! By creating an information generator, you are essentially opening the doors for more and more contact reach and campaign. By doing so you can essentially develop a new stream of revenue for your campaign, candidate, or whatever you are working towards.

Breaking The Ice Email Blast

Developing emails to break the ice can honestly be a pain. A lot of us are used to being straight to the point and very forward with our point. In an email I always suggest using a lead in email to then second that with a clean and precise sales based email. By using this method you will be attempting to use the first email to offer something your voters or donors does not have to lead them into later purchasing or subscribing to or using your service. This method has proven to have higher success rates than other methods. By giving your follower something you are almost saying in a sense " Here let me help you" or " Here let me teach you". This will resinate 10 times better than your followers that a straight to the point sales pitch! Below are 2 sample emails to show you exactly what we mean by this!

Sample A : Bad Email:

Dear John,

Vote for my guy he is thee best!

Thank You,

Joe Blow

111 Joe Blow St

(111) 111-1111

Sample B: Good Email:

Dear John,

As it is beginning to get near political season we are in need of volunteers and donors for our campaign. John is a family man and has years of experience in our local government. Please download John's FREE designed guide to fixing Will County and see what he has planned for our community!

(Click Here For Free Download)

The second email provides instructional materials as well as educational materials for the readers! By following this email and clicking on the link you will gain more FREE information. Remember that word. FREE does not always mean a giveaway. You can also give away useful content!

Chapter 6: What is a keyword and How Do I Use Them?

Now we all have heard the big scary term SEO right? If not SEO stands for search engine optimization. Yes that is a long one, but it basically means manipulating the search engine to list your website in better and or more placements. We all want our site, blog, or social media page to be seen more right? Well guess what these keywords are one of the most important things to us. Keywords control the internet believe it or not. It really does not matter which state or nation your campaign is in you are in Keywords control the ball field.

As a campaign manager, candidate or campaign webmaster unless you're that one in a million, you must put forth the effort to get the results we all want. Large campaigns now days offer positions some paying well over $100,000 a year for someone to do just that.A lot of candidates and campaigns wish to be first on the internet searches the voters and donors do. To be seen, called or sited first is huge. It takes more work and effort than most can understand. If you have ever taken a website to a top ranked spot you know exactly what I am talking about. I have worked thousands of hours over the years to develop my rankings. This is not a joke, nor a laughing matter. Building a rank via Keywords is hard work!

Keyword tricks are available. You just have to first have the basics and then secondly know how to use them to help you succeed. Keywords or phrases are often descriptive words, or title words. keeping a clean and consistent system of keywords and phrases can definitely help make a difference. If you use precise keywords and phrases you can quickly and easily gain a website or blog traffic amount that you will be proud of sharing. My blog is currently receiving 23,000 hits a day. What you may ask do I blog about? Conservative principals and events. I started it as a hobby and still only blog 3 days a week. I didn't spend thousands on marketing. I instead decided to do what I had learned over time. I watched hundreds of youtube videos, read others blogs and followed famous bloggers for years, then I put my own ideas into making this a reality. Keywords were a huge part of making my blog succeed. I learned that I could compete for

KEYWORDS and I dove in. The thought that I myself could capture a certain word on the internet was intriguing to me. I found the use of key words amazing. Using nifty tricks can always help you advance your keyword search. One of the main tricks I use is key-wording everything the same. I find a keyword that I wish to use, and then I use it on all of my tags. From basic keywords, to keywords in my photos and when I am creating content. I have found that over a few week period If I over use one word and do so more than my competitors I can overcome any keyword domination. As long as what I am key-wording is relevant and consistent I can own a word at this point.

One of the biggest questions we all must ask is what relevance does the keyword we are choosing hold to our website. If we use proper keywords, they will bring the right traffic our way. Using the wrong ones can also have an adverse effect. If you are not careful, a keyword can do as much damage as good. for instance say you are using a word such as Republican State Senate Candidate, but what you're actually promoting is a Republican State Representative candidate. You may lose control of the proper traffic. By describing what you are trying to draw traffic from to a "T" it will help you to gain traffic more efficiently than using unnecessary keywords.

Using the keyword properly can build you an arsenal of followers. Building and developing a team of followers is hard to do, but keywords will help if done properly. Defining the content you are posting is a major plus. Developing 3 strong keywords that pack a punch and using them as a back up to quality content, and a strong social media presence can develop a great ability to gain mass traffic. Mass traffic can only be useful if you as the developer or social media giant know how to use it. Using the traffic gained from keywords is difficult but can be done if you take the time to learn what all you can do with it!

Keyword research can be done simply by using google AdWords. Linking into google Adsense can build you a keyword plan. Google ranks keywords so you can see exactly how many people they hit and how they work. Using pre existing keywords that reach a large amount of people is a great starting point. Building a list of essential Keywords is important for your success in Social Media. Using social media can be extremely hard unless you have the right keys,

As we develop our site, blogs, or social media pages we will come across harder and harder tasks. Some keywords may even be used in a hashtag on our social sites. Hash tagging a word can also be extremely useful. If you're a local political PAC thats pro life in Joliet, Illinois and you use the keywords Joliet Pro Life Organization , the next time you post a photo hashtag it #ProLifeJolietIllinois. This will help viewers looking up that term to find you. A hashtag is simply a keyword associated to something you have going on with your social media page. You can use a hashtag to describe something in your photo or as a keyword to link viewers to your site.

There are various sites you can use to find the most prominent keywords for your field. A way I like to use is the simple look it up and see what is reaches. Nothing fancy, I just log onto Adsense and see where my keywords are rated. If they are rated high enough, I then use them for my site. I have always found that a bit of simple research into what you are doing can pay off tremendously!

Keywords are easy to build on as long as the Keywords you are using are solid. Once you have chosen the proper keywords we are capable of building off of them. Don't be angry if you have to beta test your keywords a few times! It's normal for up to 3 months of trials to get a proper keyword log. Using the beta testing capabilities we have can test multiple Keywords in 6 week increments. Allowing 6 weeks is usually a good amount of time to sync Keywords and see what type of traffic they are bringing.

Long Tail Keywords:

When using multiple words in one keyword such as (Aldermanic Candidate in Chicago) this is considered a long tail keyword. Developing these long tail keywords can take and a bit of research If you're a City Council in Denver and you want to dominate the long tail phrase City Council in Denver , you want to know who else is competing with you. Once you have a grasp of who pops up under your keywords you can better plan for how you are going to use certain keywords to your benefit!

If we were to build a steady stream of viewers and engagement over time at little cost, this would be our online outlet. No this will not replace ground campaign marketing, but it will help gain you a lot of traffic overtime! If you think about long tail keywords as a special voter gaining vault you will find yourself practicing the necessary steps in no time, and with consistency we will be developing a long term nest egg for your campaign and or candidate. .

Sources:

https://en.wikipedia.org/wiki/
Social_media_and_political_communication_in_the_Unite
d_States
https://www.websitehostingrating.com/instagram-statistics/

9 798602 002478